Did you hear . . .

Also by Omar Pérez, translated by Kristin Dykstra

Algo de lo sagrado / Something of the Sacred
 (Factory School, New York, 2007)

Omar Pérez

Did you hear about the
fighting cat?

translated from Spanish by
Kristin Dykstra

Shearsman Books
Exeter

First published in in the United Kingdom in 2010 by
Shearsman Books Ltd
58 Velwell Road
Exeter EX4 4LD

www.shearsman.com

ISBN 978-1-84861-132-0

Original poems copyright © Omar Pérez López, 1998
Translations copyright © Kristin Dykstra, 2010.

The right of Omar Pérez López to be identified as the author,
and of Kristin Dykstra to be identified as the translator,
of this work has been asserted by them in accordance with the
Copyrights, Designs and Patents Act of 1988.
All rights reserved.

Acknowledgements
The Spanish text of this book was first published in 1998
by Letras Cubanas, Havana.

CONTENTS

Algunos lo llaman el Juego... 6 Some call it the Game...

I. Invocación de la Albahaca 8 I. The Invocation of Basil

II. Ofrenda del puerco jíbaro 58 II. Offering of the rustic pig

145 Kristin Dykstra:
Cat vs Monument

Algunos lo llaman el Juego, otros la Flor o el Espejo. Todos coinciden en que se trata de un instrumento de mutación, como un abanico que se torna espada, luego rama, seca o en floración, luego llamarada y silencio. Un abanico de viaje.

La criatura llega a la Isla con el propósito de la mutación, sin embargo las aguas del océano amniótico le hacen olvidar. La criatura llega a la Isla sin propósito. Más tarde aprende: *praxis, poiesis, Kyrie eleison, benedictus qui venit in nomine domini. I can't give you anything but love baby, Il faut absolumment sincère*, cubanidad es amor, las mujeres mandan.

La palabra está en el juego, mas no es el juego, la moral y el ejercicio cíclico de la consciencia están en el juego, mas no son el juego. Patria es una mujer preñada de maíz, libertad es una de las contraseñas pueriles que los jugadores intercambian. La criatura practica el olvido y su cuerpo se enciende con una memoria que traspasa la Isla y el agua que la separa de otras islas. ¡Ay relámpago horizontal sobre la superficie de las aguas! ¡Ay criatura erguida en el cuerpo del relámpago!

"Es una técnica de sinceridad que comprende todas las técnicas", dijo el Hombre sobre la montaña insular.

"Quiero aprenderla", saltó la Criatura.

"Es fácil. Fija lo improvisable. Por ejemplo, un beso. Improvisa lo fijo. Por ejemplo, una montaña insular. Dale muerte al criterio".

"¿Y mis pensamientos?", clamó la Criatura.

"No te sirven de nada. Considéralos insectos sobre la corteza de un árbol en crecimiento. Eso es lo sublime del pensar, si te interesa saberlo".

"Tengo preguntas que responder", reflexionó la Criatura.

"No respondas nada. No reacciones ante las evidencias. Ahora otra Criatura te espera. Enséñale lo que has olvidado".

Some call it the Game, others the Flower or the Mirror. All agree that it deals with an instrument for mutation, a fan that becomes sword, then branch—dry or covered in flowers—then a sudden flame, then silence. A fan for a journey.

The creature arrives on the Island with the purpose of mutation, yet the waters of the amniotic ocean cause it to forget. The creature arrives on the Island without a purpose. Later it learns: *praxis, poeisis, Kyrie eleison, benedictus qui venit in nomine domini. I can't give you anything but love baby, Il faut être absolumment sincère*, Cubanness is love, women are in charge.

The word is there in the game, but it is not the game. Morality and the cyclical working of consciousness are there in the game, but they are not the game. Nation is a woman bearing corn, liberty one of the childish watchwords that the players exchange. The creature practices forgetting and its body catches flame with a memory, one that lances the Island and the water separating it from other islands. O, lightning spreading across the surface of the waters! O creature upright in the body of the lightning!

"It is a technique for sincerity that comprehends all techniques," said the Man of the island mountain.

"I want to learn it," the Creature blurted.

"It's easy. Anchor the improvisational. For example, a kiss. Improvise the anchored. For example, a mountain on an island. Deal a death blow to discernment."

"And my thoughts?" the Creature protested.

"They're worthless. Consider them insects on the bark of a growing tree. That is the sublimity of thought, if you're interested in knowing it."

"I have questions to answer," the Creature reflected.

"Don't answer anything. Don't react to proofs. Another Creature awaits you now. Show it what you have forgotten."

I.
Invocación de la albahaca

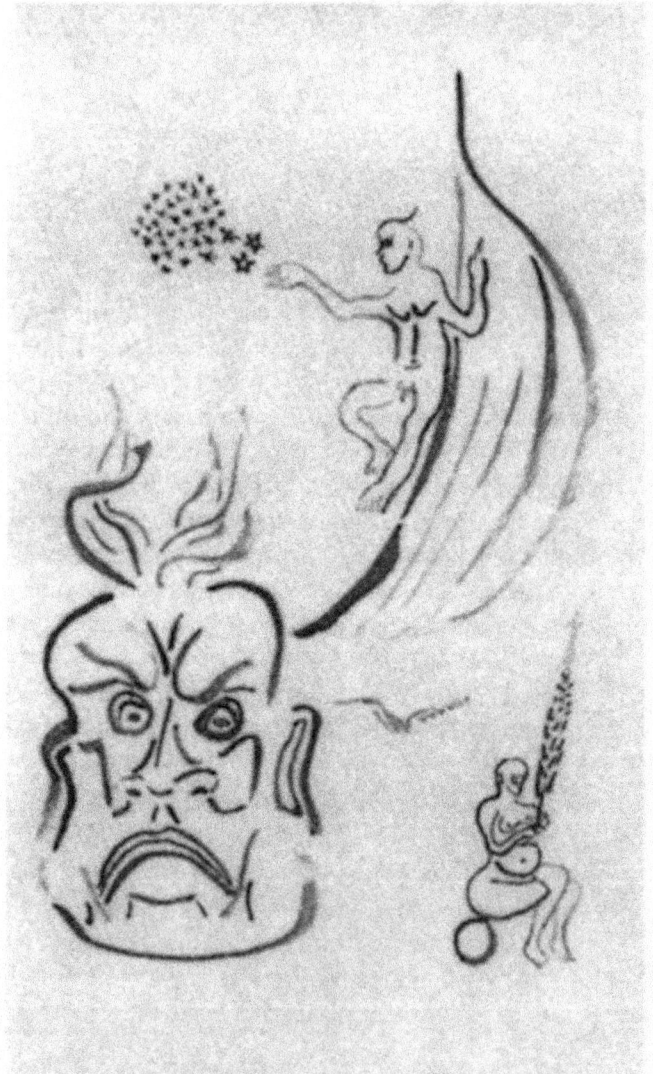

I

THE INVOCATION OF BASIL

Como su nombre Índica   os contempla orgullosa
más oscura que el jazmín   más perfumada que el aire
si tuviera que correr por los mil mundos
te llevaría en cruz bajo la lengua
déjame aquí mejor, ni planta, ni piedra, ni animal
silencio tiembla cavidad de la campana
hacer algo por la patria   deletrée consanguíneo
de flores como lunares en la mejilla del paria
si tuviera que correr por los mil mundos
cromosoma, mambo, Vía Láctea
con licencia pensamiento   Oh beata soledad
guaguancó del tiempo España   sin pecado   concebida
¡león vegetal de la escritura!
mata el deseo de correr por los mil mundos
ni flor, ni bestia, ni apero de labranza   duermo
ya no más divididos en sílabas   morir por la patria es
en su constelación los embriones
en su casita verde los espíritus
y que todo sea   para nada
y que todo sea para nada.

As her name Indiacates   she looks to you proudly
more obscure than jasmine   more perfumed than the air
if I had to race through the thousand worlds
I'd carry you on a cross under my tongue
best leave me here, not plant, nor rock, nor animal
silence quivers cavity of bell's interior
to do something for the patria   spell the blood relation
in flowers like moles across the cheek of the pariah
If I had to race through the thousand worlds
chromosome, mambo, the Milky Way
with license thought   Oh devout silence
guaguancó from Spain's time   without sin   conceived
lion of writing!, vegetal
it kills the desire to race through the thousand worlds
not a flower, not a beast, not a farming implement   I sleep
no longer divided into syllables   to die for the patria is
in their constellation the embryos
in their verdant house the spirits
and may it all be   for nothing
and may it all be for nothing.

La delicadeza engendra pánico

Delicacy fathers panic

Lo discontinuo

No siendo Adán sino un lejano sucesor
era indiferente a los nombres de las cosas:
"Al mediodía se echa sobre un rectángulo de tierra
a la sombra de la frase "soy el que soy"
que sus labios proyectan como si realizaran un tatuaje borroso
del encuentro de la luna con un gallo rojizo".

The discontinuous

Not being Adam but a distant successor
he was indifferent to names given to things:
"At noon he sprawls on a rectangle of earth
in the shadow of the phrase 'I am the one I am'
that his lips throw as if shading a blurry tattoo
twelve hours later he thinks he's the result
of the moon's encounter with a rust-colored rooster."

El miedo abreva en la ausencia de nobleza

El miedo abreva en la ausencia de nobleza
allí se queda.
Aflora entonces en las medusas, la contradicción de los trapecios
y el desenvolvimiento de las guerras.
Así como la mantis no se hace distinguir por una librea
o una emanación irritante
así como la sangre en las cavidades, aquello que fluye
no suele ni detenerse ni mostrarse.

Fear provides water in the absence of nobility

Fear provides water in the absence of nobility
that's as far as it goes.
It surfaces in jellyfish, the contraction of the trapezoids
and the self-assurance of wars.
Like the mantis it draws no attention with fine livery
or any irritating excretion;
like blood in the cavities, that which flows
neither pauses nor reveals itself.

En el estanque

El pájaro no aprende a volar en el fondo del estanque.
La línea que traza el agua en la arena movediza
no se deja reproducir en adopción
de la misma línea a mano alzada.
El rastreador la sigue con la vista en la ceniza
y se conecta con el humo del tizón apagado.

In the pond

The bird does not learn to fly on the bottom of the pond.
The line traced on quicksand by the water
cannot be reproduced by tracing
the same line with the wrist raised.
The tracker follows it, eye trained on ash,
to connect with smoke rising from extinguished embers.

Hombre,
Señor de la transfugacidad

El liquen ante el sol
la transfugacidad ante la muerte:
hombre y liquen parpadean.

Man, Lord of transfugacity

Lichen confronting sun
transience confronting death:
man and lichen blink.

Uno y diez mil

Disolver la piedra, aglutinar el polen:
cuando el hombre múltiple se desvanece
el imposible salta sobre su cuerpo agotado.

One & ten thousand

Liquefy stone, clot pollen:
When man-as-multitude disperses
man-as-impossibility jumps over his worn body.

Mi voz atiendes,
no mi conversación

Dios estoy vivo: giro en el recinto del mundo
canto tras la empalizada del cuerpo.
Tu voz, no tus estatutos, necesito.

You focus on my voice, not the art of my conversation

God I live: I turn in the encircling world
I sing within the barrier of the body
It's your voice, not your laws, that I need

¿Quién eres animal?

¿Quién eres animal?   El hombre
es la adivinanza de Dios,
Dios la del hombre.

Animal who are you?

Animal who are you?   Man
is enigma to God,
as God to man.

El león echado

La nuca sobre la rama de algodón:
el hombre se redime en su sueño.

The lion at rest

Back of the neck above the cotton branch:
in sleep man is redeemed.

Cerro Potrerillo

¿Qué eres Dios? ¿de qué color
es el hilo de araña en la neblina?

*

Efigie griega de cuarzo silencioso
dama Luna de los niños insomnes.

Cerro Potrerillo

What are you God? what shade
is spiderweb in the mist?

*

Lunar face in noiseless quartz
madam Moon to sleepless children.

Puerta Claro de Monte

Señal de gavilán en el lecho del río
panal silvestre que los hombres evitan:
Cristo se da como la mala hierba.

Puerta Claro de Monte

Sparrowhawk call on the riverbed
wild honeycomb evaded by men:
Christ gives of himself as the weed.

Final de invierno,
patio de montaña

San Isidro, tus flores
sangre sutil, espíritu compacto.

Winter's end, mountain's ground

Saint Isidore, your flowers
blood subtle, spirit close.

Inicio de primavera
en Corcovado

En la ladera desprovista de lluvia
girasoles de salvación.

**Start of spring
on Corcovado**

On the slope deprived of rain
sunflowers from salvation.

Carretera de El Macío

Debajo las luciérnagas
arriba las constelaciones
dentro, los niños de la luz.

Road to El Macío

Below, the fireflies
above, the constellations
within, the children of the light.

Peregrino de buenas maneras
Bois ton sang, Beaumanoire

Sus pies no evitan el cardo ni el estiércol:
lo llevan hasta el campo del áloe
que se espiga junto a la costa árida.

Well-mannered pilgrim
Bois ton sang, Beaumanoire

His feet avoid neither thistle nor dung:
they carry him to the field of aloe
spiking up by an arid coastline.

Uno y otro proverbio

La ofrenda de incienso
y el buitre
se encuentran en lo alto.

*

Inhalar de los proverbios
el humo que hacen cuando arden.

One proverb and another

The offering of incense
and the vulture
meet on high.

*

Inhaling proverbs
the smoke they make when they burn.

La solemnidad
de los pobres pensamientos

La solemnidad de los pobres pensamientos
varas lacustres, mangle
descortezado por el roce del ser
y sus atavíos.
Pericardio, tú alojas los pobres pensamientos
como pescadores en un lago.
La orilla, la lluvia el cardumen
son acogidos por ti, después me acogen.

The solemnity of lowly thoughts

The solemnity of lowly thoughts
lacustrine sticks, mangrove
peeled by the abrasion of presence
and its garments.
Pericardium, you shelter lowly thoughts
like fishermen at a lake.
The shore, the rain the shoal of fish
are taken in by you. Later, they take me in.

Aparejos de nacimiento
lleva María

Aparejos de nacimiento lleva María
la doncella del misterio maíz
del misterio albahaca y del misterio
Rosa María ¿no soy tu espina?
caen de ti, caen caen
caen de ti
pensamientos. ¿es eso sugestión?
Yo soy tu espina. Sobre una espina
se asientan la tempestad y el lago
sobre el lago se asienta tu óvalo de hierba:
por él me asiento. Sólo de hierbas puedo hablar
me lees, me aspiras en el trazo de la hierba quemada
y el fuego nos hace jóvenes, el humo nos hace antiguos
en el óvalo de hierba sobre el lago
en la tempestad sobre la espina
en los atavíos de nacimiento de María
que se acerca con la miel de los peregrinos.

María carries rigging for nativity

María carries rigging for nativity
maiden of corn's mystery
of basil's mystery and of the mystery
Rosa María am I not your thorn?
they fall from you they fall they fall
they fall from you:
thoughts. Is that suggestion, then?
I am your thorn. Above the thorn,
the storm and the lake settle in.
Above the lake, your oval of herbs settles in.
I sit down upon it. Only of herbs can I speak
you read me, you inhale me in the tracing of burnt grass
and the fire renders us youthful, the smoke renders us ancient
in the oval of herbs above the lake
in the storm above the thorn
in María's garments for nativity
she approaches with the honey of pilgrims.

La progresión

Cuando no basta uno, dos son necesarios
cuando no bastan dos, cuatro son necesarios
cuatro inician la progresión hacia un número
al cual llaman absurdo en las escuelas.
Pregunta: ¿Cuántos hombres son necesarios
para levantar una casa?
Respuesta: Absurdos hombres son precisos
cuanto uno no basta y dos no logran
hacer el trabajo de Uno.
Y a esos hombres ¿cuántas monedas
daremos para retribuirlos?
Absurdas monedas son precisas cuando una
partida a la mitad y repartida
no basta.
¿Y cuántas palabras se necesitan para
    transformarlos?
Absurdas y absurdas y absurdas palabras son precisas
cuando el silencio no basta.
Es esto lo que llaman progresión:
Absurdos hombres no bastan para levantar la casa
ni absurdas monedas para contentarlos
ni absurdas palabras para disuadirlos.

The progression

When one isn't enough, you need two
when two aren't enough, you need four
with four the progression begins, moving toward a number
that schoolteachers will call absurd.
Question: How many men do you need
to put up a house?
Answer: You need absurd men
when one isn't enough and two can't do
the work of One.
And how much money should we give these men
to compensate them?
You need absurd coins when one coin
sliced in half and handed out
isn't enough.
And how many words do you need to
    transform them?
Absurd and absurd and absurd words
when silence isn't enough.
This is what they call progression:
Absurd men aren't enough for putting up the house,
absurd coins don't make them happy
absurd words can't dissuade them.

Las congregaciones

Un pescador junto al otro
una gaviota junto a las otras
gaviotas sobre los pescadores.

Congregations

One fisherman alongside the other
one seagull alongside the other
seagulls over the fishermen.

Hierba, antepasado del humo

Herb, ancestor of the smoke

Otoño, mañanita

Intimación del vidrio en la llamada de lo verde
Te amo, dices, como si la prestancia
de lo dicho se abundara a sí misma
en la promesa. ¿Es abundante
lo suficiente? Sí, cuando lo dicho
nos respondía, callado, en lo santo
de una mano, de un pie
enervado por la altura del amor
mismo,
mismo amor de lo hablado en la
promesa y el vidrio y la
lechuga que el otoño levanta
de la tierra.

Autumn, very early in the morning

Hint of glass in the call of the green
I love you, you say, as if the elegance
of the thing said were abundant of itself
in the promise. Is the sufficient thing
also abundant? Yes, when the thing said
answered us, quietly, in the grace
of a hand, a foot
enervated by the heights of love
itself,
same love of which the promise
spoke, and the glass, and the
lettuce that autumn raises
out of the earth.

Como hormigas sobre un planeta casto
los pensamientos en el inicio del invierno.

Like ants on a virgin planet
thoughts at the start of winter.

II.

Ofrenda del puerco jíbaro

II.
OFFERING OF THE RUSTIC PIG

Cunda, el herrero, en el bosquecillo de mangos
ofrece al Hombre Infinito algo que comer

platos moteados de leche
pimienta, anís estrellado
para quien siega el floreciente yo
posa su pie sobre el enano
de alas de mariposa

platos cruentos, así como la mano
no vacila ante los condimentos

para el Sentado mañana y tarde
en el cráter de los nenúfares

carne impura como siempre
es la carne, cocinada
con mis ojos en sus ojos

carne de animal salvaje
proscripto como el espiritú

Y he aquí que la va aceptando
sin decir esta boca es mía.

Cunda, the metalworker, in the mango grove
offers the Infinite One something to eat

dishes speckled with milk
pepper, star aniseed
for someone who shatters the flourishing ego
who places his foot on the butterfly winged
dwarf

dishes stained with blood, like the hand
it does not falter between seasonings

for the One Sitting morning and afternoon
in the crater with water lilies

meat impure as meat
always is, cooked
with my eyes inside his eyes

flesh of wild beast
forbidden as the spirit

And here I hold that he's accepting the flesh
without saying a word of his own.

Gallo del amanecer
tampoco hoy
despertar.

Rooster of sunrise
haven't awoken today
either.

Si es coraza una pluma puede atravesarlo
Si es pluma el viento no puede arrastrarla
Si es viento no va. Tampoco viene.

If it is armor, a feather can lance it
If it's a feather, the wind cannot move it
If wind, it goes nowhere. Nor does it come back.

Durante años llevé sombrero que me protegiera de la luna
El sol lo quemó. Cabeza fresca
Durante años sombrero de sol
La luna lo pudrió. ¿Dónde está la cabeza?

For years I wore a cap to protect me from the moon
The sun burned it up. Cool head
For years, a cap for sun,
The moon rotted it out. Where's my head?

Ya no más espada blanca
Con un golpe
Me separé.

No more now white sword
With one stroke
I cut myself away.

Consumió su vida como si lo esperaran en alguna parte
Entonces renació sin impaciencia.

Conoció de las libélulas su vivir de fósforo
Su muerte de fósforo. Mas todo fue olvidado.

Su nuevo cuerpo era sólo semilla
Un pañuelo hinchado de cereales

Ni un grano despertó antes de tiempo
Ni un grano volvió a dormir después del despertar.

He devoured his life as if they were waiting for him someplace
Then he took his rebirth without impatience.

He learned from the dragonflies their matchstick life
Their matchstick death. But all was forgotten.

His new body was simply seed
A kerchief rounded with grain

Not one germ awoke before its time
Not one germ slept again after awakening.

El pájaro siempre regresa a la madera

Bird always returns to timber

Acontecer del derrumbe:
sigo una mariposa amarilla.

Event of the collapse:
I dog a yellow butterfly.

Echado en la postura del león
mi cuerpo abarca el mundo
y tres tablas de pino.

Dropped into the lion position
my body spans the world
and three pine planks.

Kosen

Escucha amigo mío la palabra del Rey
¿Quién lo vio por las calles? Y él
¿a quién vio? Regaló un plátano al hombre
y un durazno al discípulo.
Y quién puede decir "he terminado"
quién podrá decir "he bebido".
Una escuela vacía
Una jarra vacía.

*

Pediré al marino
su chalupa, su cobre
su candil.

Kosen

Listen, my friend, to the word of the King
Who saw him going through the streets? And he,
who did he see? He presented the man with a banana
and the disciple with a peach.
And who can say "I have finished"
who will be able to say "I drank."
An empty school
an empty jar.

*

I'll ask of the sailor
his skiff, his copper
his lantern.

Buda de Corcovado

En la prolongación de la sequía
limpio como un piso de tierra
recto como la sombra de la mantis.

Buddha of Corcovado

During the continuation of the drought
clean as the earthen floor
straight as the shadow cast by the mantis.

Estrella fugaz, verte es el deseo

Fleet star, desire is to see you

Solo, como el gato en mi regazo
¿adónde van de noche los girasoles?

Lonely, like the cat on my lap,
where do the sunflowers go at night?

Incienso prende
para atisbar en el incendio.

Incense catches light
for sighting in the blaze.

Imprecaciones, adivinanzas

No en balde ardía.

*

Se absorbe a veces con el humo perfumado
un poco de ceniza.

*

¿Mirar adónde antes de cruzar?
Atravesaré como un perro cansado.

*

En cuanto a mí
divino blasfemar.

*

Rutina del misterio
imposible sin ella.

*

Los gatos a la vía
los santos a su ataúd.

Imprecations, perplexities

Not in vain did it burn.

*

Sometimes with perfumed smoke you take in
a bit of ash.

*

Look where before crossing?
I'll move across like a tired dog.

*

For my part
to blaspheme is divine.

*

Mystery's routine
impossible without it.

*

The cats to their alley
the saints to their coffin.

Gran baile, no se mueve

Great dance, doesn't move

María del Pilar

Oh tú pan de junio
cal fresca y avellana
del sacrificio estela
del intercambio síntoma y frutilla
Oh pan de azogue
nudo y deslizarse
Enloquecen así
sólo los dioses.

María del Pilar

Oh you bread in June
fresh lime and hazelnut
from the sacrifice a wake
from exchange, symptom and berry
Oh bread of quicksilver
crux and slither away
They go mad like this,
only they, the gods.

Cráneo, cazoleta de álamo
no mereces que en tu ladera crezca el lirio salvaje
pero crece.

Cranium, cedar basin
you don't deserve to have a wild lily grow along your slope
but it's growing.

Saludo de los perros

Al llagado, al que produce llagas
al que las cura
tantos granos de maíz tostado en el cuenco de la luna
tantas luciérnagas en el tronco del flamboyán, infectado
los perros, los olvidados príncipes
los guerreros echados de la casa del colibrí
no más guerra al cuerpo que tiembla sin comprender
al pensamiento que piensa sin especular
al hombre-perro en el espejo del corazón
no más tratados
estiremos el espinazo hasta la galaxia más próxima
orinemos al pie de los volcanes
para revivir el magma se dan hierbas amargas
un mechón de carretera antigua
una oración a la Virgen María Despalilladora
diecisiete centavos en un tazón de piedra.

Greeting from the dogs

To the one with sores, to the one who makes the sores
to the one who cures them
so many kernels of corn toasted in the hollow of the moon
so many fireflies in the trunk of the flamboyán when it's infected
the dogs, forgotten princes
warriors expelled from hummingbird's court
no more of war to the body that shivers uncomprehending
to the thinking that thinks without speculation
to the man-dog in the mirror of the heart
no more of treaties
let's stretch our spines toward the closest galaxy
piss on the feet of the volcanoes
to revive their magma, a gift of bitter herbs
a lantern from the ancient road
a prayer to the Virgin Mary as Tobacco Worker
seventeen cents in a bowl of stone.

Las instituciones místicas
del decoro

Hay un tigre que mira la televisión
sabe mirar lo que en el ojo se aquieta:
el paso
miríadas de peces en el manto estelar
luna que se quiebra   como el pan de Cristo
comemos de ese pan y de la luna
y los supuestos sobre los cuáles
toda la vida se asienta y fija
allí orina el tigre
no para delimitar ni poseer
fecunda el humus universal
siente el hocico de nueva criatura aproximarse
orina entonces.
A lomos de tigre la princesa Vida
cabalga la noche de pétalos
de azucenas, dices   o tal vez de aquellas mil
diminutas azucenas reunidas en tu mano
ellas también sin nombre. Mas a fuerza de nombrar
conozco, olvido, me aproximo:
vida, azucena, sangre   y patria aún
al combate corred como la espuma
¡Cómo! sonríes   yaguaza sobre tigre
candil en el sepulcro de los dioses   muchachita
patria es.

*

Las puertas son del corazón las manos
no son herméticas, mi sangre
amplias, acuchilladas puertas

The mystical institutions
of decorum

There's a tiger watching television
he knows how to watch the thing that grows calm inside his eye:
the flow
myriad fish in the mantle of stars
moon that breaks   like the bread of Christ
we eat of the bread and moon
and the suppositions on which
all of life is built, is fixed:
there the tiger urinates
not to mark or to own
but to make the universal humus fertile
he senses the snout of a new creature arriving,
he urinates then.
Riding the tiger, princess Life
jockeys the night with its
lily petals, you say   or maybe with those thousand
diminutive Madonna lilies gathered in your hand,
similarly nameless. Well through the force of giving it a name
I come to know, come to forget, come closer:
life, lily, blood   and patria even
hurry into combat, like the surf
What! You smile   our duck the *yaguaza* rides the tiger
oil lamp in the sepulcher of the gods   girl
that's patria.

*

The hands are the doors to the heart,
are not inscrutable, blood of mine
the wide, knife-stabbed doors

Uno, dos, tres   corazón aquí
haya un tercer corazón   ahora escucha.

*

Padezco un decoro encendido
Nube, llévate mi luz
Hay tanta capacidad en la nube
para captar la luz
Luna, aquiétala
Magnolia   no recuerdo
mas si nos aproxima   sea.

*

Goce de lo sublime
en árbol, pan, libro, escarcha
¿para qué?
el amor   anestesia.

*

Escucha el tercer corazón   escucha
el mío   se desenvuelve en lirio africano
en espuma de niños se concentra
Escucho el tuyo   playa retoza
camino de profundidad leñosa flor señala
en el vientre de encendida virgen
y encendida virgen nos contempla.

*

One, two, three   here heart
Maybe a third heart   now listen.

*

I suffer through a form of decorum, flushed
Cloud, take my light
There's so much room in the cloud
for capturing her, the light
Moon, calm her
Magnolia   I can't remember
but if she comes close to us   let it be so.

*

Pleasure from the sublimity
in tree, bread, book, frost
what for?
love   anesthesia.

*

Listen to the third heart   listen
Mine   opens into an African lily
concentrates into a surf of children
Listen to yours   beach frolic
way of profundity woody flower signifies
on the womb of flushed virgin
and flushed virgin she is gazing at us.

*

Guaguancó Santos Suárez

Pensamiento del deseo, no te puedo desear.
Cuando el poeta llegó a territorio sagrado
traía el olfato encantado y patas de gato fino
A Santos Suárez llegó   Santos Suárez Tamarindo
A Santos Suárez llegó   buena sombra lo cobija
Era desorden divino y arrebato sosegado
encontró panal de abejas, ceiba alta y dulcería
unos dicen la Gran Vía, otros dicen timbiriche
cazó paloma rabiche, ojos de cerveza oscura
No quiero premeditar, pues una vida pensada
es lo mismo ante la Nada que una vida sin pensar
A Tamarindo llegó   mundo nuevo la gitana
A Tamarindo llegó   camposanto parquecito
Yo no sé si ante el deseo el imposible aparece
no quiere crecer y crece   yerbabuena
me parece   que de un cuenco los deseos se derraman
Invisible
A Tamarindo llegó   campana la Milagrosa
En Santos Suárez no sé si me van a sepultar
si me voy a desposar en templo de caracoles
si las estrellas son soles y un sol un copo de nieve
Santos Suárez cómo llueve   A Tamarindo llegó
Milagro vuela bajito   A Tamarindo llegó
Yo no sé si la gaviota tiene razón al volar
si le cogió el gusto al mar o se enamoró del cielo
Santos Suárez mi consuelo   A Tamarindo llegó
Que no te pesen las alas   A Tamarindo llegó
Santos Suárez la gaviota   mambo.

Santos Suárez Guaguancó

Constant dwelling on desire, I cannot desire you.
When the poet arrived at the sacred place
he brought a dainty cat pace and an enchanted nose
To Santos Suárez he came   Santos Suárez Tamarind
To Santos Suárez he came   fine shadow at his order
It was divine disorder, paroxysm in repose
he found honeycomb, tall trees and a *dulcería*
was that shop the Gran Vía, or was it just some little dive,
looked for a mourning dove with eyes of dark beer
No planning ahead here see a life lived in thought
is the same thing to Nothingness as life lived unthought
To Tamarind he came   new world, gypsy woman
To Tamarind he came   tiny park, graveyard   don't know
if the impossible shows when faced with desire
it doesn't want to grow but it grows, spreads like mint
I think I know: our desires dribble from the bowl
Invisible!
And to Tamarind he came   to its cathedral bell
Don't know if they'll bury me in Santos Suárez
if I'll marry underneath the church's conch shell
if stars are suns, and a sun, a ball of snow
Santos Suárez, the rain blows!   to Tamarind he came
Miracle flies low   to Tamarind he came
I still don't know if the dove is right to fly
whether she fell for the sea, or is falling in the sky
Santos Suárez my reason why   to Tamarind he came
and may your wings not weigh down   to Tamarind he came
Santos Suárez sea dove,   mambo.

Sentado inmóvil
en el mundo a mis espaldas
¡hasta las aves de corral me dicen adiós!

Sitting motionless
in the world at my back
Even the poultry wishes me goodbye!

La mutación

¿El caracol es vacío o lleno
abierto o cerrado?
soplo en él, en él respiro:
bocina de nave.

Blanca la nave recoge el mugido nupcial
Llora el niño que ha nacido en el no pensamiento
recién nacido el pensamiento
¡Bienvenido!

Dos moscas temblando
se posan sobre mi vientre al mediodía.

Mutation

Is the conch shell vacant or complete
opened or closed?
I blow into the shell, into the shell I breathe:
some ship's foghorn.

In white this nave captures matrimonial mooing
Cries from the child born into noncognition
Newly born, cognition
Welcome!

Two flies quivering
alight on my abdomen at noonday.

Labios, puente
descargar en el puente
Émbolo, pistilo,
polen
recoger, diseminar   qué más da
Lamer, émbolo polen   cuidado
¿de qué?   Lengua, lenguaje
estelar   tiemblo, nos estiramos
crecer, decrecer   brincar   trepar
procrear   qué alivio
sólo saliva   mundo nuevo.

These lips, a bridge
now unloading on the bridge
A piston, a pistil,
pollen
collecting, disseminating   so what
Licking, a piston   pollen   be careful
of what?   the tongue, palaver
sidereal   I tremble, we extend ourselves
expanding, declining   bobbing   climbing
procreating   well that's a relief
simply saliva   novel world.

Dojo

Una isla en el coro
Una isla en el polo
Vegetación: "hombres rebeldes y cordiales"
Método, el Abrupto: luz
Luz y caballero Bodhidharma.
¡Hasta la bandera quedó bajo la lluvia!
¿y yo? ¡salvando moscas de la taza de vino!
El hombre del madero está en la puerta.
El hombre del madero está ya en la puerta.

Dojo

An island in the choir
An island at the pole
Vegetation: "rebellious and cordial men"
Method, the Suddenness: light
The light, and genteel Bodhidharma.
Even the flag was left out there in the rain!
and I? rescuing flies from the wineglass!
The wooden man is in the doorway.
Now the wooden man is in the doorway.

Desayuno en el infierno
almuerzo en el paraíso
a la noche los ojos se me cierran.

I breakfast in hell
I lunch in paradise
my eyes close hard at night.

Saliva, pensamiento
empujo con la nuca las ventanas del dharma.

Saliva, thinking
with the nape of my neck I push the dharma windows.

Sangha

Bienvenido a la iglesia de los locos
Manolo, Ryokan, cabo de hacha
o machete, ¿Gauloises?, ¡bien *sûr*!
A la puerta del bosque los zapatos.

Sangha

Welcome to the church of the insane
Manolo, Ryokan, battle axe
or machete, Gauloises?, bien *sûr*!
Shoes by the doorway to the forest.

Extremo espiritú

Eh, el espiritú
Eh, el elegido, ¡eh!
Extenderlo en el hecho extremo   eh
No tiene puntos cardinales.

Extreme essence

Eh, the essence
Eh, the elect, eh!
Extending it to the extreme event   eh
It enjoys no cardinal points.

Catarsis: Idea central

¿Pero purificación entendida   cómo?
como si por los siglos de los siglos
rechazar la identificación: identificarse con el rechazo
Hombre, desfila en la transformación
Tú, el principal.

Catharsis: Main idea

But purification understood how?
for centuries of the centuries as
rejecting identification: identifying yourself with rejection
Man, step on through transformation,
You, the main character.

Cuerpo magistral

¿Qué sería de mí sin el cuerpo?
de ti sin el cuerpo
cuerpo de la enseñanza
La Verdad: suculenta
        carne humana
Estómago: la compasión
aerodinámica:
¿Cómo, para quién, la transacción?

Body of the master

What would be of me without my body?
of you without your body
body of learning
The Truth: succulent
        human flesh
Stomach: compassion
aerodynamically:
The transaction, how? and for whom?

Cintio

Tenemos un amigo en común: nadie
el oso tras la constelación
el filamento en la rosa
los mil filamentos
las esporas no pueden evitarse
Nadie puede evitarlas, no las evita
¿Los apóstoles? Nadie el apóstol
un soplo siempre fuera de lugar
encaja siempre en nadie
la siempreviva.

Cintio

We have a mutual friend: nobody
the bear behind the constellation
filament on the rose
the thousand filaments
the spores can't be evaded
Nobody can evade them, and does not evade them
Apostles? Nobody the apostle
a puff of air always dislocated,
the miracle plant everlastingly fit
into nobody

El árbol del ataúd

Con la madera de este árbol, ataúd
con la madera del ataúd, pira
en la pira crece hasta cero el hombre
¿ahora qué hacemos?

The coffin tree

With the wood from this tree, coffin
with the wood from the coffin, pyre
on the pyre man grows toward zero
so what do we do now?

Muchacho al fin

En tu pecho los campos de arroz
observados desde Ícaro
embrión hasta la victoria siempre
en el callejón sin salida de lo eterno
¡Muchacho al fin!
eres la mosca que revolotea en la pirámide
eres también la pirámide.

At the end a boy

On your chest the fields of corn
seen by Icarus
embryo moving always toward victory
down the alley with no exit to eternity
At the end a boy!
you are the fly who flutters in the pyramid
you are also the pyramid.

La guajira metafísica

Tú, vacío funcional
variantes del voltaje, única luz
Efecto perecedero del Amor
luces diversas
Sostén
Sosténlas
las sostienes.

The metaphysical countrygirl

You, functional space
variants in voltage, the only light
Transitory effect of Love
several different lights
Sustain
Sustain them
you sustain them.

Fin de la moral

Brindo con un poco de mi vinagre preferido
el acabóse, ¿cómo contaminarlo?
Todo apetito el hombre
cigarro tras cigarro
baila tras la cocina
baladas de contención
¡Horizonte, el invierno se va!

End of the moral

Raising a cup of my favorite vinegar
here's to final chaos; how can I contaminate it?
All appetite, is man
cigar after cigar
he dances toward the kitchen
ballads of containment
Horizon, winter's on its way out!

sopla, sopla, pero no era ceniza
sino un insecto
Vuela.

puff, puff, but that wasn't ash
it was an insect
And flying.

Sesshin

Ni siquiera los Budas escapan a los mosquitos
¿Qué comer? ¿cómo dormir? ¿para qué todo esto?
El guardián de la ermita dice:
"Soy prácticamente un ser humano".

Sesshin

Not even the Buddhas escape mosquitos
What is there to eat? how do I sleep? why bother with all this?
The chapel guardian says
"I'm practically human."

Iniciación a las escalas
un beso: revoluciones
la técnica no está en los libros.

Initiation to musical scales
a kiss: revolutions
the technique can't be found in books.

Mi bandera. Composición

Al volver a distante ribera donde el niño
se cose a la idea fija
¡a los creyones!: sangre, jazmín y azulejo
en los departamentos: Nueva York, Manicaragua, Coliseo
Paso Quemado, San Leopoldo donde brilla
la Estrella, ciruela china de los libertadores.
Del cafeto un árabe plantó en Contramaestre
cagadilla de abeja, a degüello en la vereda congo
No más de cien palabras, ni menos de cuarenta
¿Incinerar solemnemente?
No. La cosemos, la lavamos,
y en la pechera del Negro la prendemos.

My flag. Composition

Returning to that distant shore where the child
stitches himself to a set idea
get the crayons!: Blood, jasmine, and bluebird
in the departments: New York, Manicaragua, Coliseo,
Paso Quemado, in San Leopoldo where the Star
shines, the liberators' Chinese plum.
From the coffee tree an Arab planted in Contramaestre
a mead shat by Cuban bees, to a massacre in the Congo district
No more than a hundred words, nor less than forty
Do we burn the flag with solemnity?
No. We sew it up, we wash it up,
and on the chest of the Black Man we pin it up.

El incienso de Bárbara

Quiero cejar
y escapar
pero no lo permite el incienso de Bárbara
El Antemano fijado
quemado
por ambos lados.
Shin Mainichikhoh
cuadrado
color hierba de invierno en la ermita
de Bárbara.

Barbara's incense

I want to give up
and get out
but Barbara's incense won't allow it
The Before-hand fastened down
burned
from both ends.
Shin Mainichikoh
squared
color of grass wintering in Barbara's
chapel.

Cat vs. Monument

Did You Hear About the Fighting Cat? is the first English-language translation of *¿Oiste hablar del gato de pelea?*, the second book of poems from Omar Pérez López. Published in Cuba in 1998, the collection represented a turn in his writing that took many of his contemporaries by surprise.

Before any books of his poetry were published, Pérez (b. Havana, 1964) worked as a journalist and cultural critic for *El caimán barbudo* in the late 1980s, then as a columnist and editor with *La naranja dulce* in 1989–1990. He edited an alternative poetry magazine, *Mantis*, from 1994 to 1996. His talent for language had also led him to study English, which he began to use as a translator.

His first book of poetry appeared in 1996. In keeping with its title, *Algo de lo sagrado* (*Something of the Sacred*), it captures a sense of many things lying just beyond the reach of human language. Poems from this first collection address concerns about the relation of the individual to the nation, for example through public ritual and education. The book is also shaped by very personal issues, including the discovery of his identity as a son, a process which followed from learning his father's name.

Pérez landed on a boundary between spheres of "revolutionary" life in Cuba: one, the everyday reality of a citizen; and another, a world of modern iconology circling around images of heroism and chaos. Like it or not, he has to dedicate energy to negotiating his cultural location, which I would propose is not only unusual but unique.[1]

It is fitting, then, that he experiments with the boundaries and contents of national culture on his own resolutely unique terms. Each poetic project he undertakes reveals a new emphasis. Working with him over time, I've often spoken to other Cuban writers and critics who say they wish he would write more works like the much-anthologized *Algo de lo sagrado*. Instead Pérez has

---

[1] See 'Gossiping Cuba: Omar Pérez and the Name of the Father' in *Jacket* 35 (Early 2008) for details, including remarks from Pérez, plus quotations from a historian and other creative writers who have incorporated him into their own works as a result of this situation.

opted to keep moving and shifting directions. In short remarks which appear in various genres, he emphasizes the value of that which is contingent, open to growth and change, actively searching for new knowledge.

His turn to Zen Buddhism provided a path to follow into his second collection of poetry, *¿Oiste hablar del gato de pelea?* (*Did You Hear About the Fighting Cat?*), and onward into a more recent manuscript: a book of days, entitled Cubanology.[2] For some people, this turn to Buddhism was incomprehensible, foreign, a willful act of irrelevance or a loss of artistic direction. For others, however, the new work holds their respect. Pérez is not the only writer or artist who ever found meditation fascinating. Moreover, three of his fellow poets in Havana made a point of telling me, in 2010, that they respect his resistance of expectations from Havana's literary community. They see it as his necessary claim to the right to grow and change as a poet, an artist, an intellect, and a person.

A careful read of *Did You Hear About the Fighting Cat?* and Cubanology shows that Pérez has not simply dropped his early interest in symbols of nation, ritual, education, and masculinity. Rather he has spun new variations. He has also developed interests in interdisciplinary expression, including overlaps with music and dance. And while he does not want to write poetry that seems intellectual at the expense of art, it will be clear to anyone who reads across his works that he has been elaborating related ideas across genres.[3]

I once asked Pérez why he chose a title about a fighting cat for this book. He answered, "Have you ever tried to make a cat fight when it didn't want to?" The spirit of resistance and

---

[2] *Cubanology* is still unpublished as of this writing in mid-2010. It has three layers of existence already: as a handwritten journal that Pérez carried for several years; as a manuscript typed into the computer, which he is revising; and as a translation in progress that I am carrying out.

[3] Pérez won the National Critics' Prize for the Essay in 2000. I've translated some of his later essays into English. "The Zen Dojo in Havana" is the translation of a 2001 essay (see *Origin~* Longhouse, Sixth Series, No. 4 [2007]: 132-149). "The Intellectual and Power in Cuba" is based on an original essay from 2005 (*Fascicle* 3 [Winter 06-07]).

reflection is there, on the surface, intertwined with awareness of a gossiping community. Inside there are at least two traditions in play.

On one level, *Did You Hear About the Fighting Cat?* is a book of meditation informed by Zen traditions of interrogating "enlightenment." It is a quest narrative, a pilgrimage of mind and body. Poems suggest survival of daunting conditions, press questions about what we really need in life, and register the turning of the seasons. In keeping with the spirit of this interrogation, ephemerality and nothingness get more interest from Pérez than monuments.

Another important aspect of the book is its play on national culture, so often referenced in the construction of literal and figurative monuments. The Spanish-language poems elaborate tension between sameness and change by absorbing phrases used in Cuba. In one of the first poems, for example, there's a mysterious woman who looks proudly at "you."[4] She is not a mystery for anyone who recognizes her as a feminized Cuba from the island's national anthem. Its original melody, the "Himno de Bayamo," was composed by Perucho Figueredo in 1867. At that time Cubans were involved in independence struggles against Spain. Figueredo added words to the hymn in 1868 after an important defeat of Spaniards by revolutionaries at Bayamo, a city in eastern Cuba. The song instructs Bayameses—patriots—to hasten to battle: dying for the expectant patria (homeland) means living. That lesson is firmly redacted in the beginning of *Did You Hear About the Fighting Cat?*, and other poems periodically gesture at patria before a final return to its "set idea." There's plenty of reference to Cuban culture in this book for those who seek it, though as the treatment of the anthem illustrates, monuments may be opened to deconstruction, dematerialization.

Pérez continued to explore connections between Zen Buddhism, Cuban life, and his own interests years after this book first appeared. He attended sesshins organized by French master Stéphane Thibaut[5] in Havana, then pursued an opportunity to

---

[4] Pérez has further played on the word 'indicar' for extra meaning, thus the unusual spelling used in English.

[5] Thibaut's name as a monk is Kosen, which became the title of a poem in this book.

visit Europe, which allowed him to attend camps with the master and to practice with diverse groups who gathered in dojos. He completed his training as a Zen monk and was ordained. Pérez also fell in love with a woman and lived with her in Amsterdam from spring 2002 through fall 2005, periodically visiting family in Cuba as he struggled to make ends meet in Europe. He wondered whether he should plan to stay in Europe or return to the island. Thoughts of staying, hopes for good employment and residency, and his romantic relationship eventually fell through. Pérez returned to live in Havana with a new set of experiences and perspectives.

Overall, Zen Buddhism was very important to Pérez and his own writing for an important section of his life and career. He specifies that he prefers to consider Zen a basis for practice rather than spiritual adherence. Given the right teacher, meditation and dialogue can become a way to negotiate with ideas and experience, which he contrasts to the passive acceptance of any system.

One day he was thinking about how *one* might best position *oneself* in relation to Ernesto "Che" Guevara, who like the nineteenth-century poet and revolutionary José Martí is almost exaggeratedly iconic as a thinker in Cuba and abroad. Pérez took out his book of days and wrote,

> With some beings, it's advisable to look them in the eye—not to look upwards from one's knees like a devotee, nor to stand like a tourist facing a monument. Much less looking downwards from the height of a moral construct turning one, in the end, into the conscious or unconscious accomplice of a system and civilization erected over all manner of crimes, commonly written off today as accidents or necessary evils.

This distanced phrasing comes from *one* who has felt his own body turning into an abstraction of public discourse. Based on our most recent conversations, it is also a good description of his attitude toward Zen after more than a decade of meditation and writing.

Pérez won Cuba's Nicolás Guillén Prize for Poetry for *Crítica de la razón puta* in late 2009. In 2010 he is moving forward with a different phase of daily life and literary experimentation. *Lingua Franca*, published this spring, is multilingual; he has composed a series of poems in English, a collection he calls *common nonsense*. Pérez is also turning toward more frequent engagement with music. If you've ever wondered what a *reggueton* might look like if composed by an experimental poet-translator-essayist-carpenter-Zen-monk, you're in luck.

Kristin Dykstra

Acknowledgments: Earlier versions of these translations appeared in *Washington Square*, *Origin*~Longhouse, *Jacket*, and *Mandorla*.

Kristin Dykstra's translations and commentary are featured in bilingual editions of poetry by Reina María Rodríguez and Omar Pérez, including *Algo de lo sagrado / Something of the Sacred*. With Kent Johnson, she organized a dossier of work by Pérez for *Jacket* 35 (Early 2008) with an interview, translated poetry from two projects, two critical essays and other resources. Among her other translations are poems and essays by Cuban writers Ángel Escobar, Juan Carlos Flores, Rito Ramón Aroche, Pedro Marqués, and Efraín Rodríguez. Dykstra co-edits *Mandorla: New Writing from the Americas* with Gabriel Bernal Granados (MX) and Roberto Tejada (USA). She is Associate Professor of English at Illinois State University.

www.ingramcontent.com/pod-product-compliance
Lightning Source LLC
Chambersburg PA
CBHW031149160426
43193CB00008B/311